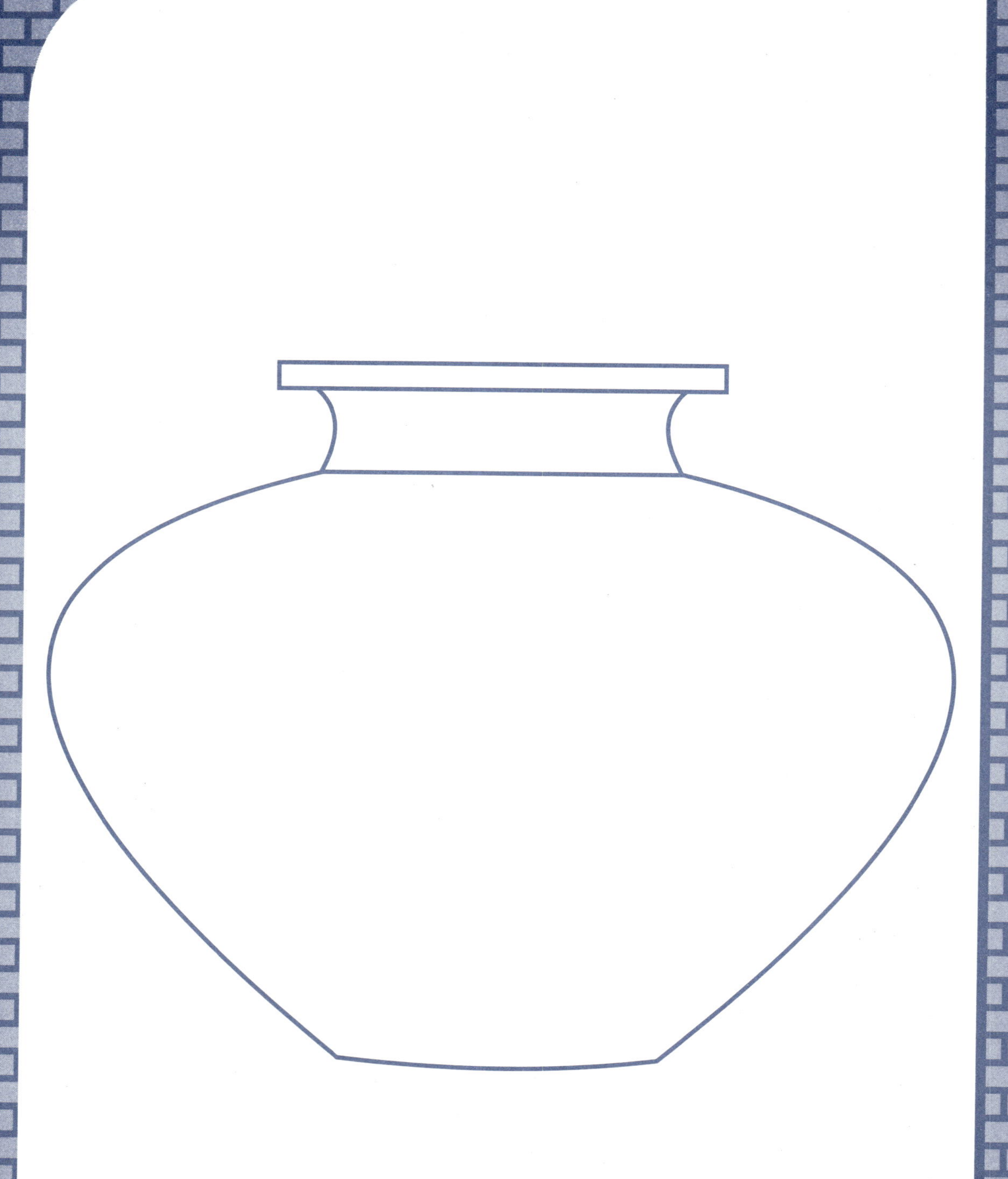

FUN WITH COLORS

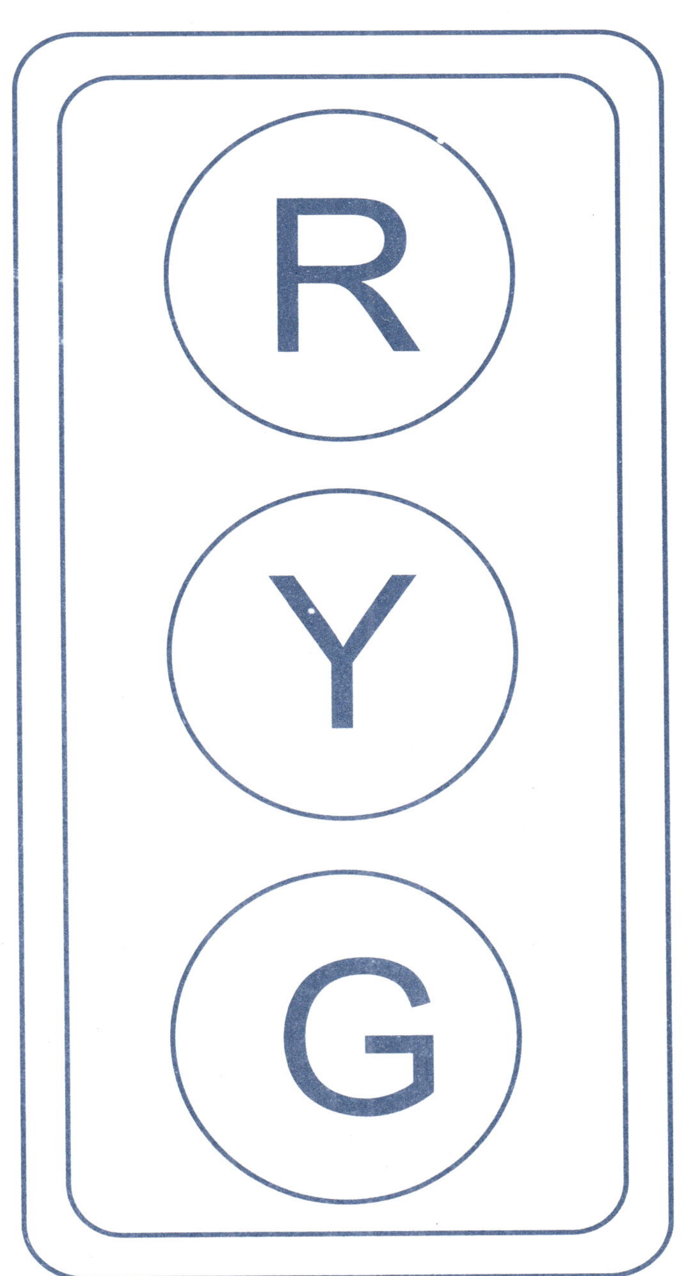
R
Y
G

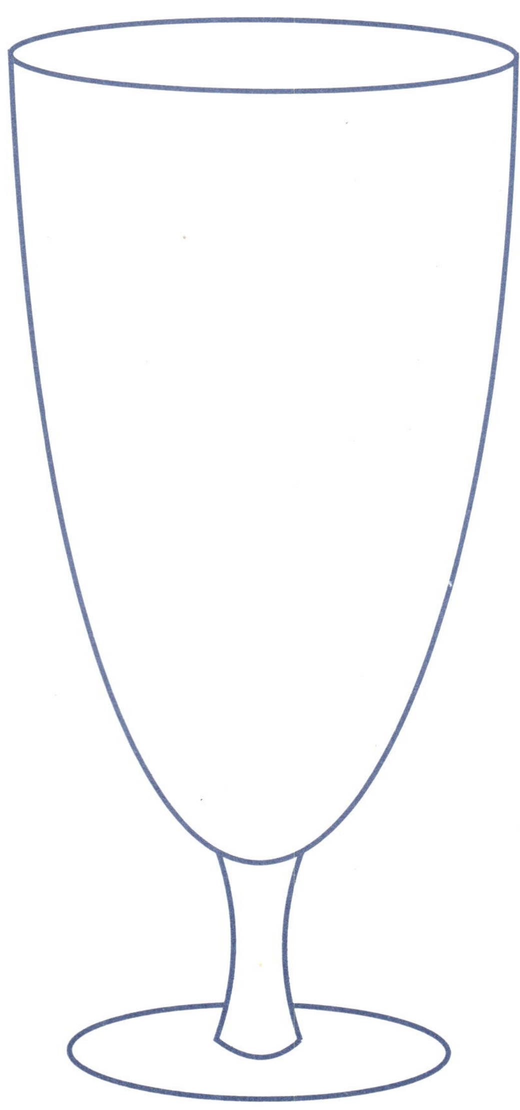

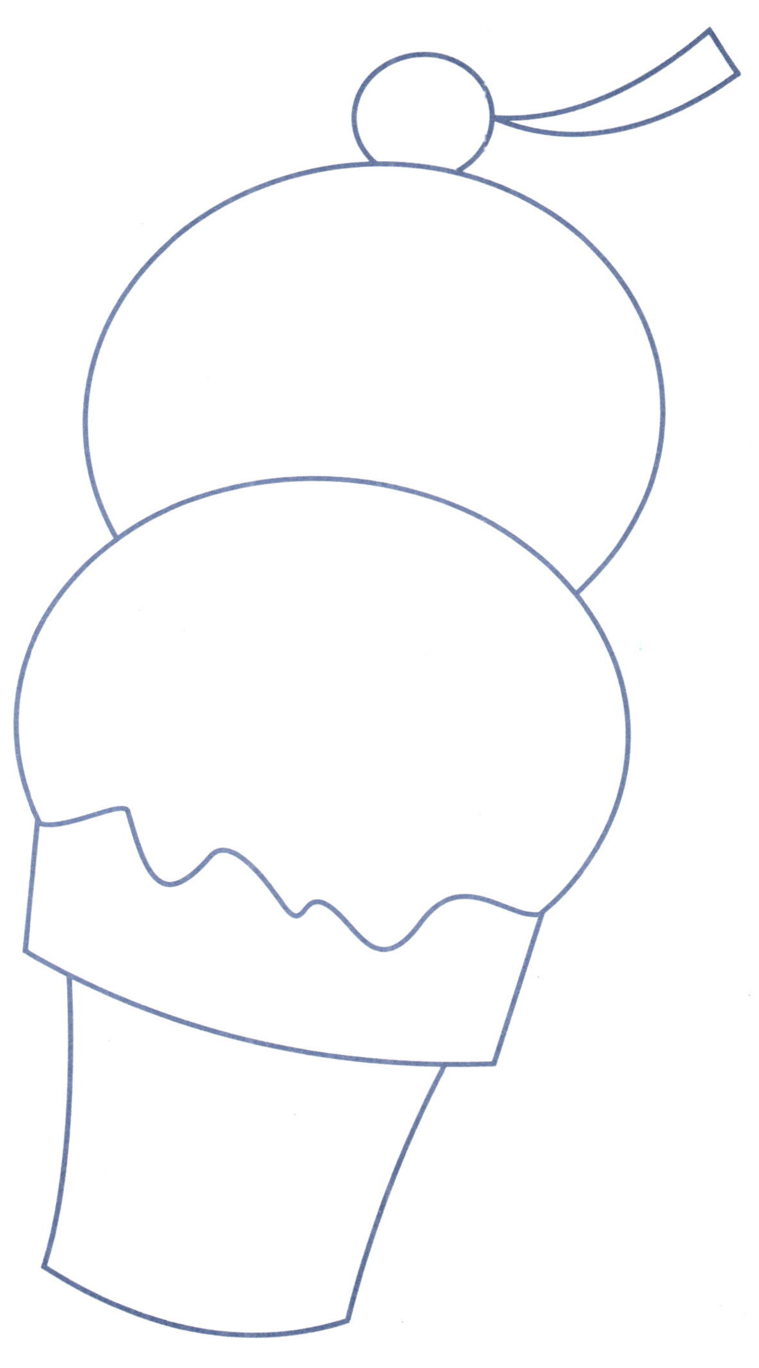

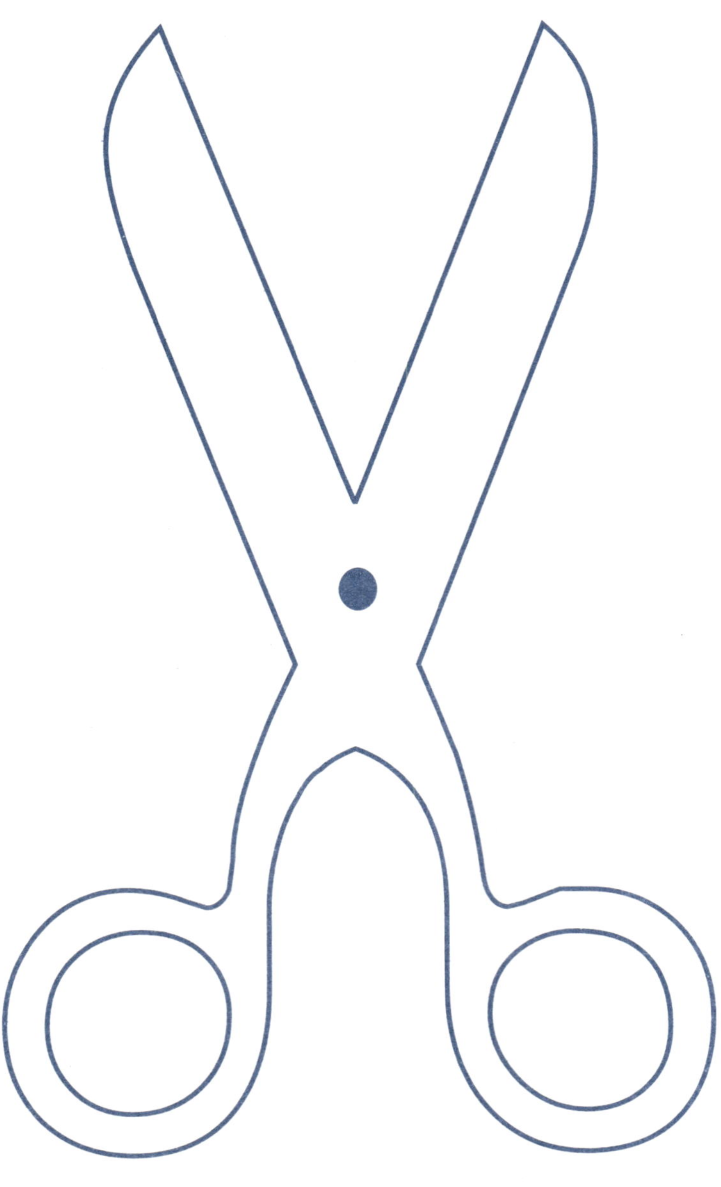

FUN WITH COLORS

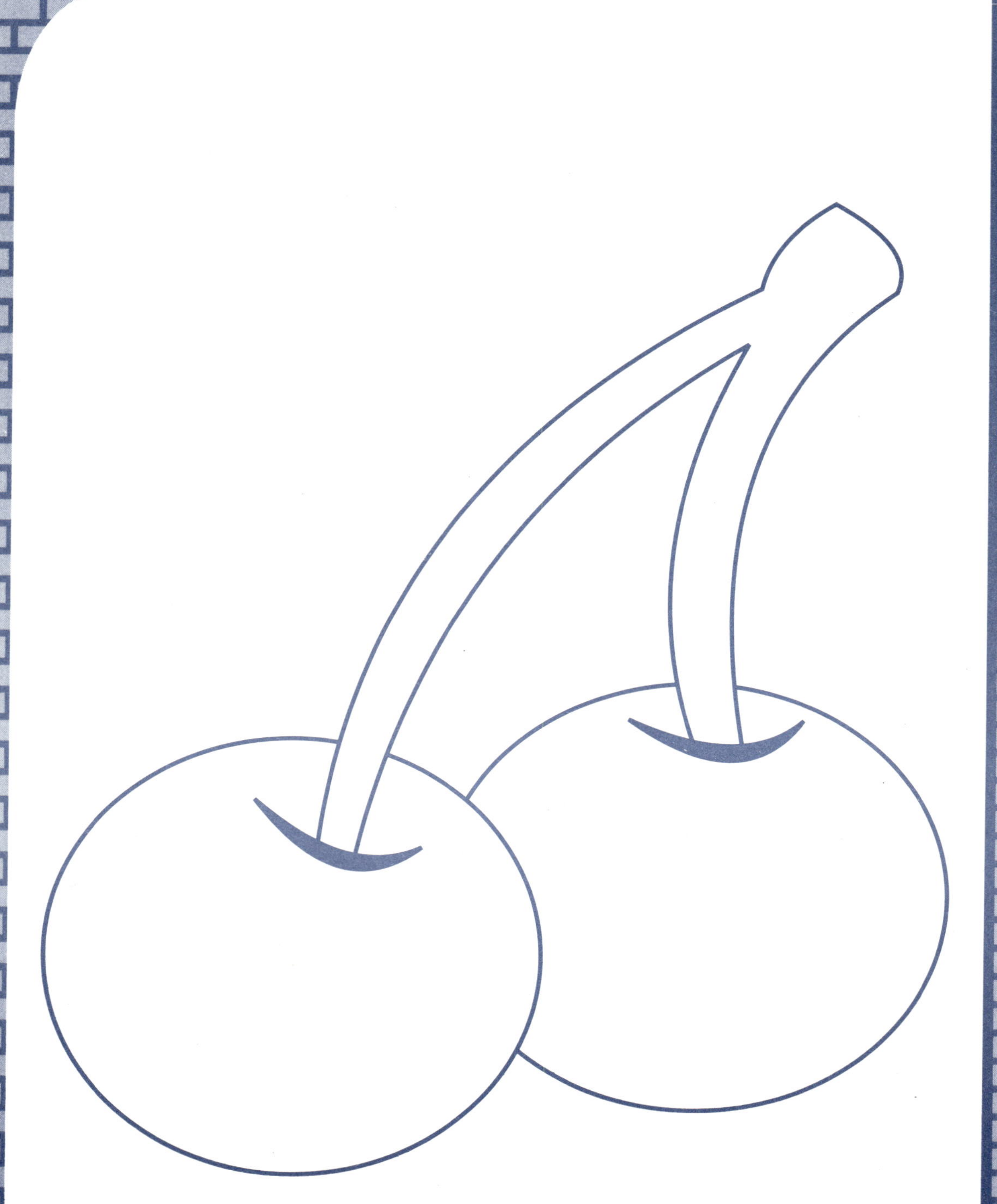

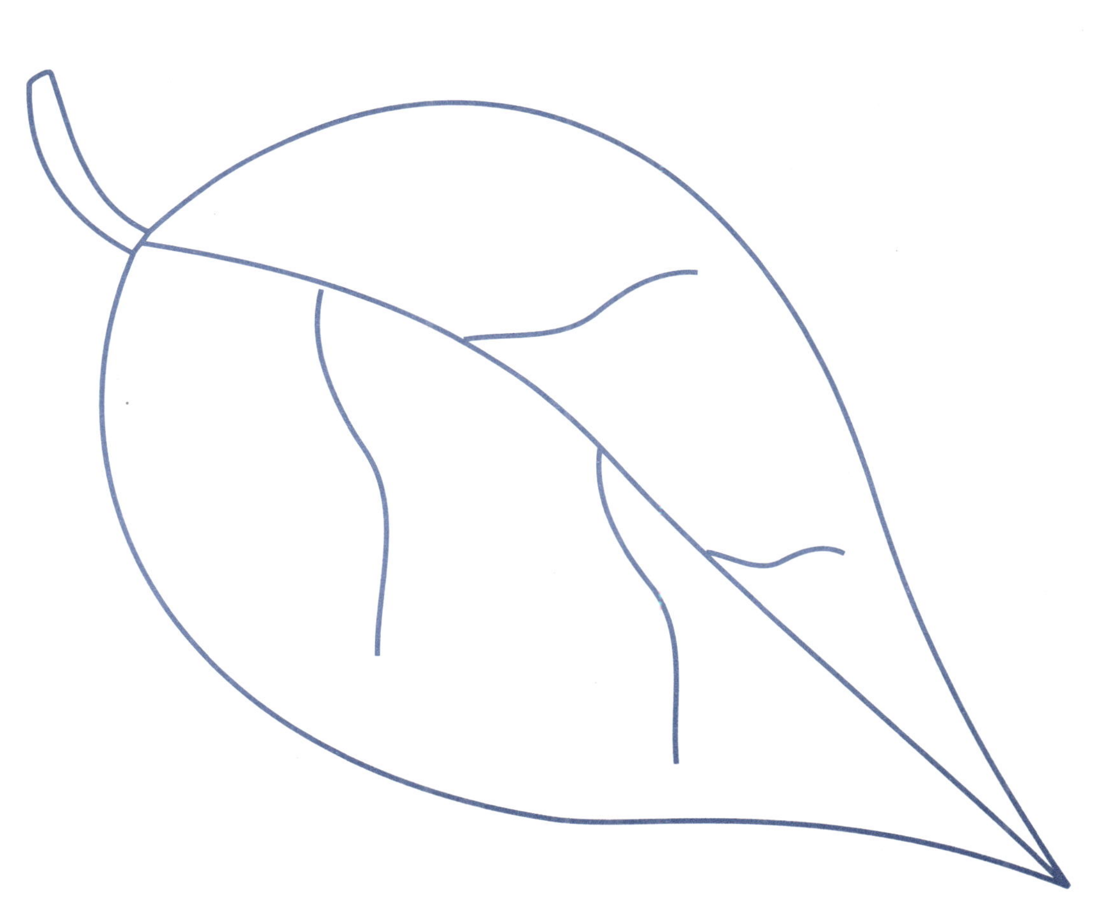

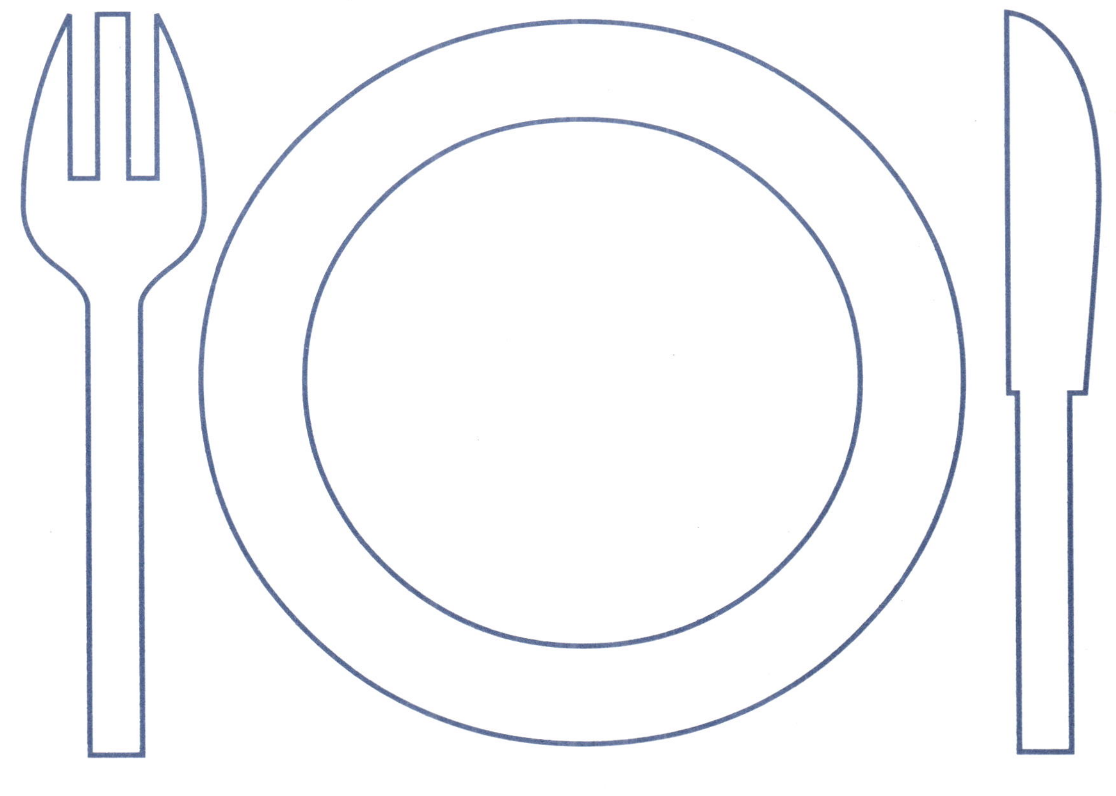

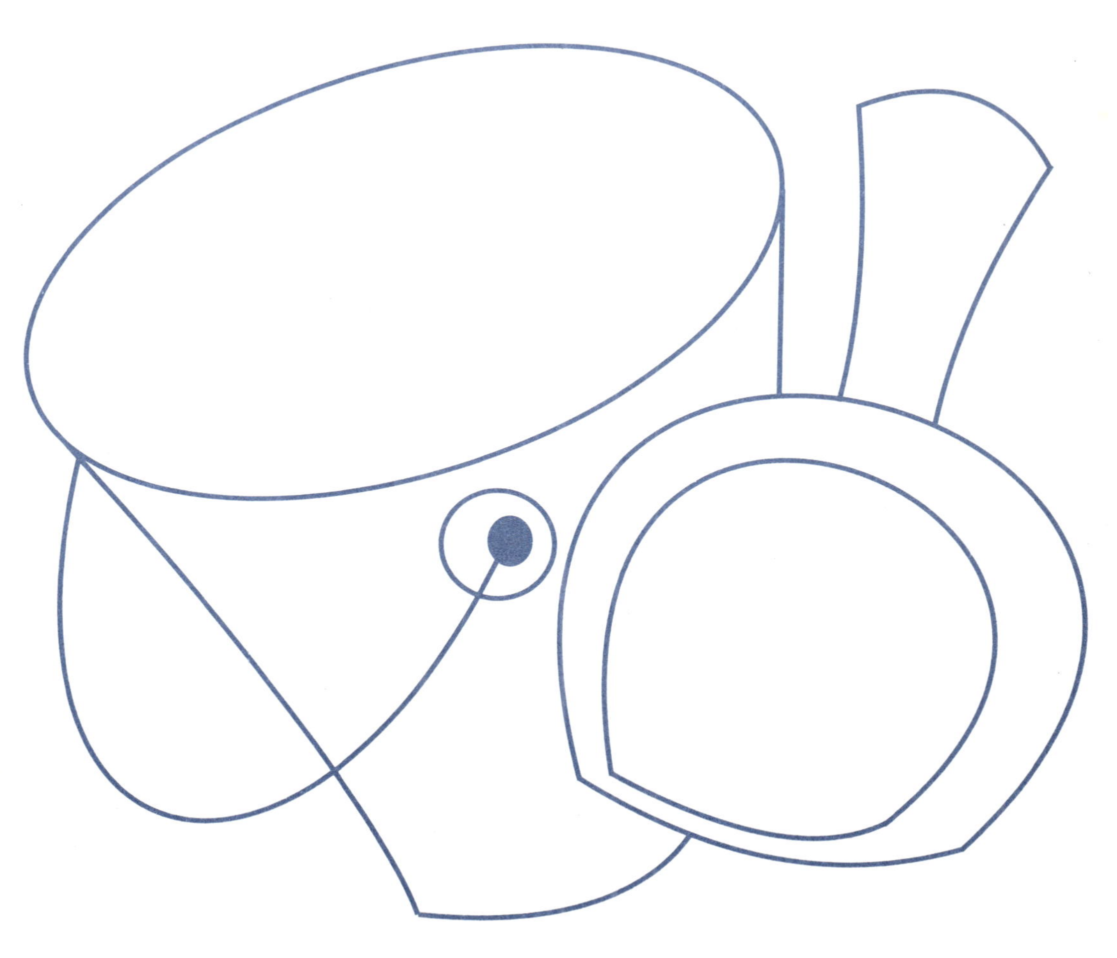

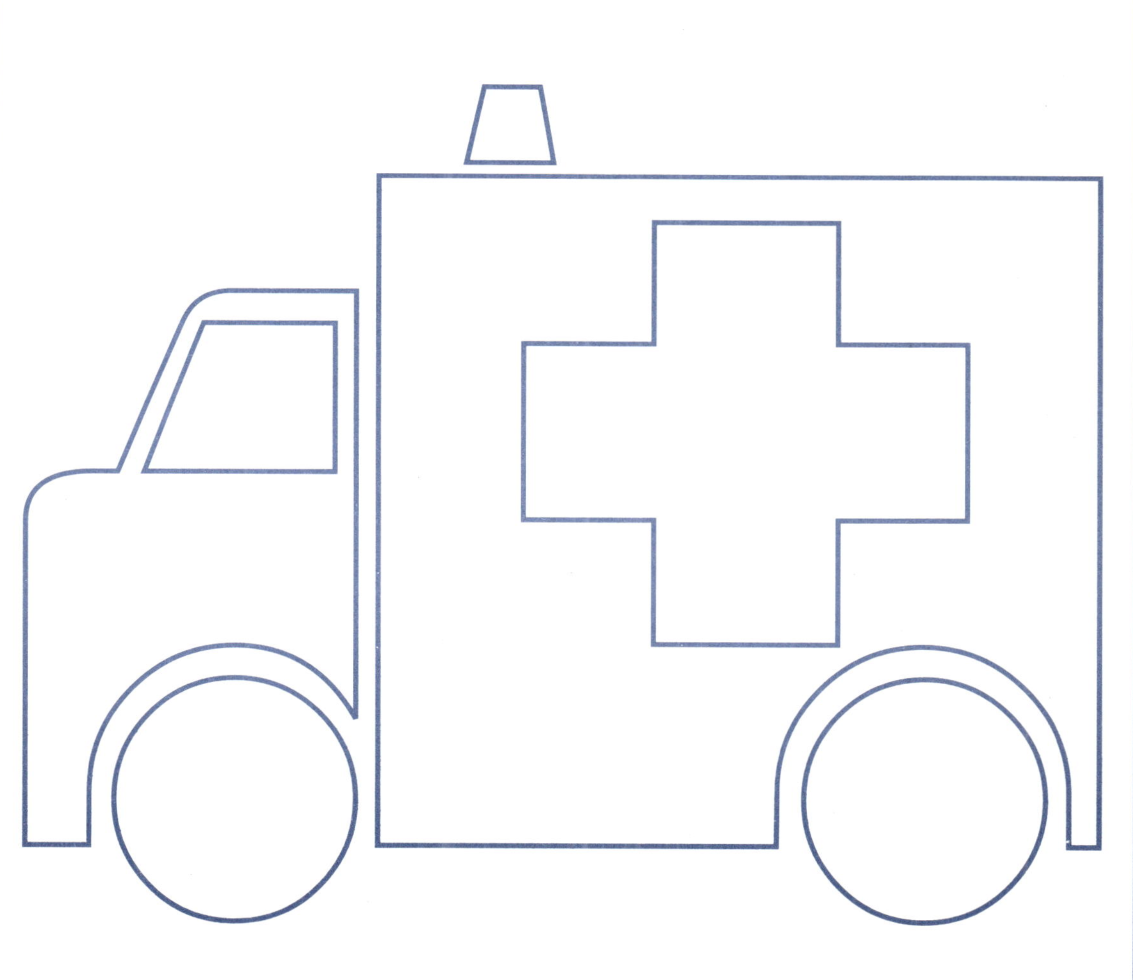

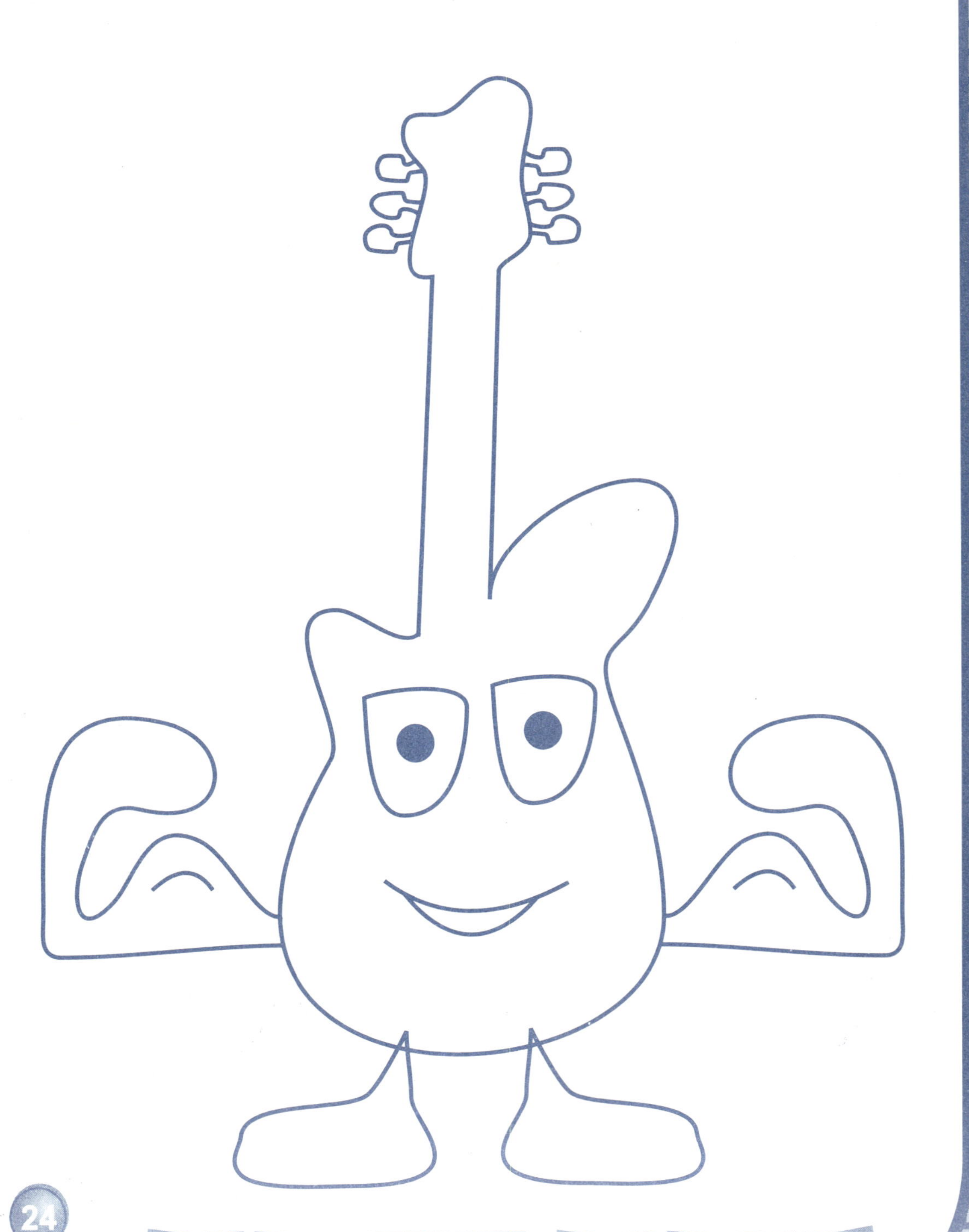

FUN WITH COLORS

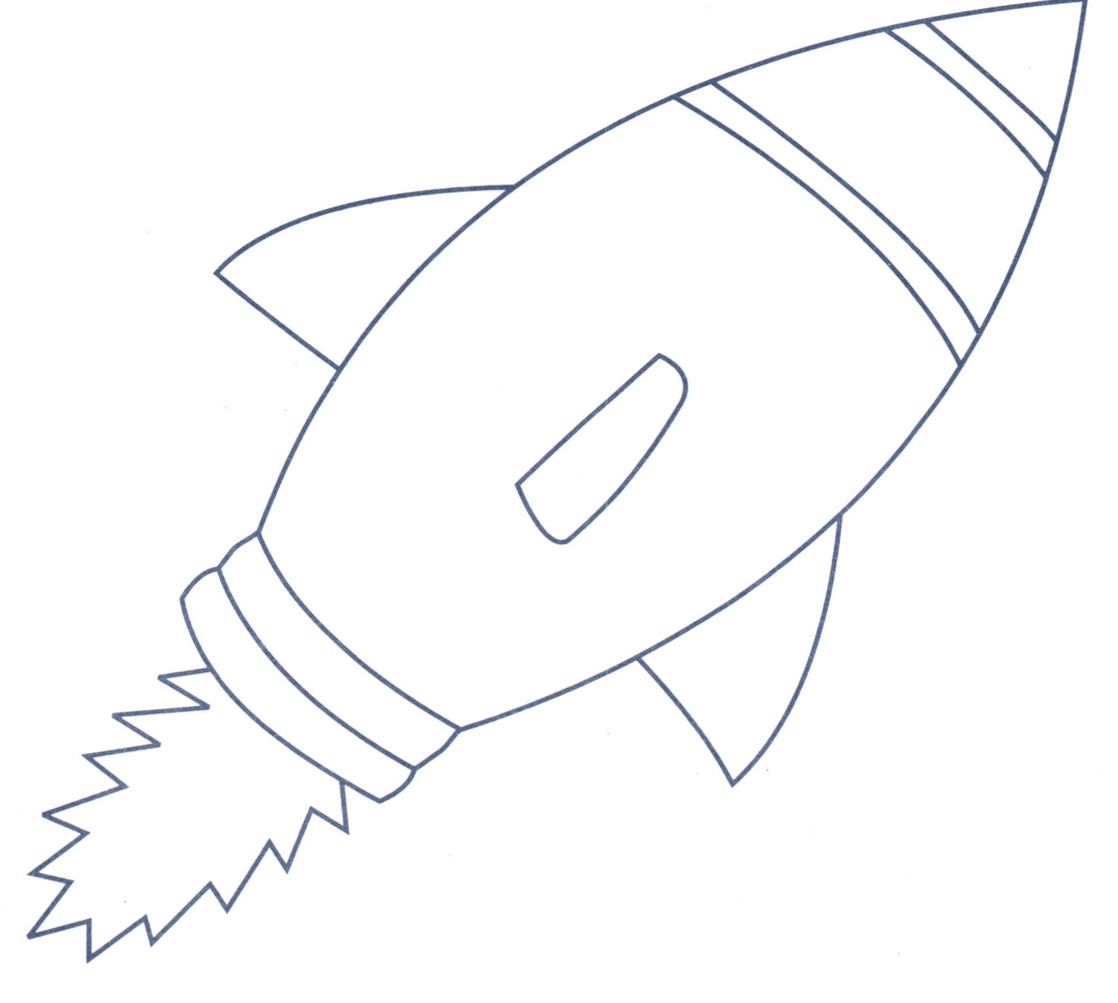